HOME & HEART IMPROVEMENT FOR MEN

BY CYRANO DE WORDS-U-LAC

Honor Books
Tulsa, Oklahoma

Unless otherwise indicated, all scripture quotations are taken from the *Holy Bible, New International Version* ®, NIV ®, Copyright © 1973, 1978, 1984 by International Bible Society. Used by permission of Zondervan Publishing House. All rights reserved.
Scriptures marked KJV are taken from the *King James Version* of the Bible.

2nd Printing
Over 26,000 in Print

Home & Heart Improvement For Men

ISBN 1-56292-208-4
Copyright © 1996 Dan & Dave Davidson
Rhymeo Ink
P.O. Box 1416
Salem, Virginia 24153

Application Has been made for a registered trademark for "Rhymeo" and "Show-It Poet."

Published by **Honor Books, Inc.**
P.O. Box 55388
Tulsa, Oklahoma 74155

DEDICATED TO
OUR FATHER-IN-LAWS,
PAUL RUSE AND JERRY VAN WYK,
VISIONARIES FOR THE LORD AND
TRUE MEN OF INTEGRITY.

WHAT'S A RHYMEO™?

RHYMEOS™ ARE FAT-FREE UN-POETRY — LITE AND LEAN LITERARY CUISINE. RHYMEOS™ ARE SHORT AND SKETCHY, QUICK AND CATCHY — TWO SHORT LINES REINFORCED IN RHYME. ALTHOUGH THE SHORT RHYMING COUPLETS DISPLAY A POETIC FLAVOR, THEY ARE NOT TRADITIONAL POETRY. THEY ARE ACTUALLY JINGLES ABOUT LIFE — JINGLE VERSE POETRY FOR THE 21ST CENTURY — OFFERING INSIGHT AND MOTIVATION, HUMOR AND INSPIRATION.

CYRANO DE WORDS-U-LAC PENS THE SHORTEST VERSE IN THE UNIVERSE — A STORY TO TELL IN A NUTSHELL, A RHYMING REPORT TO MAKE A LONG STORY SHORT. RHYMEOS™ ARE SHORT AND SWEET AND POETICALLY PETITE — CLEVER WAYS TO PARAPHRASE — BITE-SIZED WORDS TO THE WISE. WHETHER CONCISE ADVICE OR AN EASY DOESY FUZZY WUZZY, RHYMEOS™ GIVE A REFLECTIVE PERSPECTIVE IN A FIRESIDE CHAT FORMAT. IT'S LITERARY RAP WITH A SNAP — POETICALLY CORRECT DIALECT — A WAY TO COPE WITH HUMOR AND HOPE!

I PROMISE

TO HONOR GOD THROUGH INTERCESSION
WORSHIP, OBEDIENCE AND CONFESSION;
HOLDING TRUE AS A MAN OF HIS WORD
TO COVENANTS OTHERS HAVE HEARD;
TAKING THE ROLE OF RESPONSIBILITY
AND BROTHERLY ACCOUNTABILITY.

I PROMISE

TO DEMONSTRATE INTEGRITY,
WITH MORAL AND SEXUAL PURITY;
GIVING TO MY CHILDREN A SAMPLE
OF GOD'S LOVE AND GRACE BY EXAMPLE;
MAKING MARRIAGE AND FAMILY A PRIORITY,
HONORING MY WIFE AND PROVIDING SECURITY.

I PROMISE

TO REACH OUT BROTHER TO BROTHER IN GRACE
REGARDLESS OF DENOMINATION OR RACE;
WITH AMBITION AND FAITHFUL VISION
TO FULFILL THE CHURCH'S MISSION;
PRAYING DAILY TO ALWAYS BE
THE MAN GOD MADE ME.

BY CYRANO DE WORDS-U-LAC

SERVE THE LORD AS YOUR REWARD.

1 Corinthians 3:14
If what he has built survives,
he will receive his reward.

CHOOSE THE OPTION OF GOD'S ADOPTION.

Romans 6:8
Now if we died with Christ,
we believe that we will
also live with him.

NEVER IN VAIN, TAKE GOD'S NAME.

Deuteronomy 5:11
You shall not misuse the
name of the LORD your God.

LAY UP TREASURE
IN HEAVENLY MEASURE.

Matthew 6:21
For where your treasure is,
there your heart will be also.

KNOCK AND THE DOOR WILL BE OPENED ONCE MORE.

Matthew 7:7
Ask and it will be given to you;
seek and you will find; knock and the door
will be opened to you.

IN GRACE KNOW
HOW TO GROW.

2 Peter 3:18
But grow in the grace and knowledge
of our Lord and Savior Jesus Christ.
To him be glory both now and forever! Amen.

PLAN TO PRAY EVERY DAY.

Luke 5:16
But Jesus often withdrew
to lonely places and prayed.

LIKE DANIEL, DECIDE
IN PRAYER TO ABIDE.

Daniel 6:10
...Three times a day he got down on his knees and prayed,
giving thanks to his God, just as he had done before.

GIVE GOD PRAISE
ALL YOUR DAYS.

Psalm 68:19
Praise be to the LORD,
to God our Savior, who daily bears our burdens.

WHEN IT'S HARD TO COPE, IN THE LORD HAVE HOPE.

Psalm 71:14
But as for me, I will always have hope;
I will praise you more and more.

MAKE TRUST A MUST.

Romans 10:11
As the Scripture says,
"Anyone who trusts in him
will never be put to shame."

BE RISEN
FROM SIN'S PRISON.

Romans 6:4
...Just as Christ was raised from the dead
through the glory of the Father,
we too may live a new life.

LEARN THE LESSON FOUND IN CONFESSION.

Romans 10:9
That if you confess with your mouth,
"Jesus is Lord," and believe in your heart that God
raised him from the dead, you will be saved.

HAVE A PRAYER PLAN TO FIGHT LIKE A MAN.

James 5:16
...The prayer of a righteous man
is powerful and effective.

DEVELOP A THIRST
FOR FAITH THINGS FIRST.

2 Corinthians 5:7
We live by faith,
not by sight.

BELIEVE SINS ARE ERASED BY GOD'S GRACE.

Ephesians 2:8,9
For it is by grace you have been saved, through faith —
and this not from yourselves, it is the gift of God —
not by works, so that no one can boast.

ACCEPT LOVE'S PRICE OF HIS SACRIFICE.

1 Corinthians 6:20
You were bought at a price.
Therefore honor God with your body.

SURRENDER
TO FAITH'S DEFENDER.

Hebrews 12:2
Let us fix our eyes on Jesus, the author and
perfecter of our faith, who for the joy set before him
endured the cross, scorning its shame, and sat
down at the right hand of the throne of God.

BE TEACHABLE AND PREACHABLE.

Hebrews 13:7
Remember your leaders, who spoke the word
of God to you. Consider the outcome of
their way of life and imitate their faith.

FOLLOW THE GOLDEN RULE, NOT THE FOLLY OF A FOOL.

Luke 6:31
Do to others as you would
have them do to you.

HELP MEN DISCERN DOCTRINE.

1 Timothy 4:16
Watch your life and doctrine closely.
Persevere in them, because if you do,
you will save both yourself and your hearers.

KEEP A MENTOR'S CREED IN PRAYER AND DEED.

Hebrews 10:24
And let us consider how we may spur
one another on toward love and good deeds.

TAME YOUR TONGUE WHETHER OLD OR YOUNG.

James 3:10
Out of the same mouth come praise and
cursing. My brothers, this should not be.

FLEE
THE ENEMY.

2 Timothy 2:22
Flee the evil desires of youth, and pursue
righteousness, faith, love and peace, along with
those who call on the Lord out of a pure heart.

BE A GOOD SPORT AND ALWAYS EXHORT.

Romans 15:5
May the God who gives endurance
and encouragement give you a spirit of unity
among yourselves as you follow Christ Jesus.

SHOW A SMILE
IN TIMES OF TRIAL.

James 1:2
Consider it pure joy, my brothers,
whenever you face trials of many kinds.

BE A TRAILBLAZER AND A PEOPLE PRAISER.

1 Thessalonians 5:11
Therefore encourage one another
and build each other up....

SHARE PRAYER AND REPORT WITH A GROUP OF SUPPORT.

Proverbs 27:17
As iron sharpens iron,
so one man sharpens another.

GIVE OTHERS A SAMPLE OF GOD'S LOVE BY EXAMPLE.

John 13:15
I have set you an example
that you should do as I have done for you.

BE ONE TO CONFIDE FOR OTHERS HURTING INSIDE.

2 Corinthians 1:3,4
Praise be to the God and Father of our Lord
Jesus Christ, the Father of compassion and the God
of all comfort, who comforts us in all our troubles,
so that we can comfort those in any trouble with
the comfort we ourselves have received from God.

HAVE INTEGRITY IN THE NITTY-GRITTY.

Job 27:5
...I will not deny my integrity.

BE STRONG
TO ADMIT WRONG.

James 5:16
Therefore confess your sins to
each other and pray for each other....

SET YOUR MIND ON THINGS DIVINE.

Colossians 3:2
Set your minds on things above,
not on earthly things.

KNOW THAT TO REAP, WE SOW TO KEEP.

Galatians 6:7
Do not be deceived:
God cannot be mocked.
A man reaps what he sows.

BE HUMBLE
WHEN YOU STUMBLE.

1 Peter 5:6
Humble yourselves,
therefore, under God's mighty hand,
that he may lift you up in due time.

BE A WORD DOER SO DECEPTIONS ARE FEWER.

James 1:22
Do not merely listen to the word,
and so deceive yourselves.
Do what it says.

KEEP YOUR EYES ON THE PRIZE.

Philippians 3:14
I press on toward the goal to win
the prize for which God has called me
heavenward in Christ Jesus.

DETERMINE THE DIVINE, THEN DRAW A LINE.

Isaiah 28:17
I will make justice the measuring line
and righteousness the plumb line.

WORK HARD
TO KEEP YOUR GUARD.

1 Corinthians 16:13,14
Be on your guard; stand firm in the faith;
be men of courage; be strong.
Do everything in love.

PURSUE
WHAT IS TRUE.

1 Timothy 6:11
But you, man of God, flee
from all this, and pursue righteousness,
godliness, faith, love, endurance and gentleness.

DEVELOP THE DISCIPLINE OF NOT GIVING UP OR IN.

Galatians 6:9
Let us not become weary in doing good,
for at the proper time we will reap
a harvest if we do not give up.

BE SURE
YOU ARE PURE.

Matthew 5:8
Blessed are the pure in heart,
for they will see God.

STAND FIRM
AND DON'T SQUIRM.

1 Corinthians 15:58
Therefore, my dear brothers, stand firm.
Let nothing move you. Always give yourselves
fully to the work of the Lord, because you know
that your labor in the Lord is not in vain.

AVOID THE THORN OF PORN.

Psalm 119:9
How can a young man keep his way pure?
By living according to your word.

DON'T DEVISE LITTLE LIES.

Proverbs 24:28
Do not testify against
your neighbor without cause,
or use your lips to deceive.

BE AN ORIGINAL INDIVIDUAL.

Psalm 139:14
I praise you because I am fearfully
and wonderfully made.

REACT RIGHT IN GOD'S SIGHT.

Proverbs 16:2
All a man's ways seem innocent to him,
but motives are weighed by the LORD.

REMEMBER HONESTY IS THE BEST POLICY.

Proverbs 24:26
An honest answer
is like a kiss on the lips.

DECIDE TO DECLINE GETTING DRUNK ON WINE.

Ephesians 5:18
Do not get drunk on wine,
which leads to debauchery.
Instead, be filled with the Spirit.

AVOID A PHONY TESTIMONY.

Proverbs 12:17
A truthful witness gives honest testimony,
but a false witness tells lies.

DON'T BE LUKEWARM DURING A STORM.

Matthew 8:26
He [Jesus] replied, "You of little faith, why are you so afraid?" Then he got up and rebuked the winds and the waves, and it was completely calm.

DON'T LET SIN FIND A PLACE IN YOUR MIND.

2 Corinthians 10:5
...We take captive every thought
to make it obedient to Christ.

NEVER GAMBLE OR BET A VALUABLE ASSET.

Proverbs 21:5
The plans of the diligent lead to profit
as surely as haste leads to poverty.

DEVELOP THE TRAIT TO PATIENTLY WAIT.

James 5:7
Be patient, then, brothers, until the Lord's coming.
See how the farmer waits for the land to yield its valuable
crop and how patient he is for the autumn and spring rains.

DEMONSTRATE INTEGRITY EVEN WHEN OTHERS CANNOT SEE.

Ecclesiastes 12:14
For God will bring every deed into judgment,
including every hidden thing, whether it is good or evil.

BE AN EXCEPTION
TO DECEPTION.

2 Corinthians 4:2
...We do not use deception,
nor do we distort the word of God.

SHUN THE PITCHES
OF QUICK RICHES.

1 Timothy 6:9
People who want to get rich fall into temptation
and a trap and into many foolish and harmful desires
that plunge men into ruin and destruction.

DON'T ASSUME
IN THE LOCKER ROOM.

Ephesians 4:29
Do not let any unwholesome talk come out of your mouths,
but only what is helpful for building others up according
to their needs, that it may benefit those who listen.

ZIP YOUR LIP
TO NIP GOSSIP.

Proverbs 26:20
Without wood a fire goes out;
without gossip a quarrel dies down.

AS A BROTHER,
LOVE ONE ANOTHER.

Romans 12:10
Be devoted to one another in brotherly love.
Honor one another above yourselves.

WITH YOUR EYES, DON'T IDOLIZE.

Exodus 20:4
You shall not make for yourself an idol
in the form of anything in heaven above or
on the earth beneath or in the waters below.

BE A BELIEVER
AND DODGE THE DECEIVER.

1 Peter 5:8,9
Be self-controlled and alert. Your enemy the devil
prowls around like a roaring lion looking for someone
to devour. Resist him, standing firm in the faith....

STAND UP TALL TO AVOID A FALL.

1 Corinthians 10:13
And God is faithful; he will not let you
be tempted beyond what you can bear. But when
you are tempted, he will also provide a way out
so that you can stand up under it.

GUARD YOUR HEART BEFORE SIN GETS A START.

Proverbs 4:23
Above all else, guard your heart,
for it is the wellspring of life.

DELIGHT IN WHAT'S RIGHT.

Psalm 37:4
Delight yourself in the LORD
and he will give you the desires of your heart.

ALWAYS INVEST IN WHAT STANDS THE TEST.

Ecclesiastes 12:13
Now all has been heard; here is the
conclusion of the matter: Fear God and keep
his commandments, for this is the whole duty of man.

LEAVE LUST IN THE DUST.

Job 31:1
"I made a covenant with my eyes
not to look lustfully at a girl."

KEEP PROMISES SPOKEN UNBROKEN.

Deuteronomy 23:23
Whatever your lips utter you must be sure to do,
because you made your vow freely to the LORD
your God with your own mouth.

WORK TO AVOID BEING UNEMPLOYED.

Proverbs 14:23
All hard work brings a profit,
but mere talk leads only to poverty.

BE A PROVIDER, NOT A BACKSLIDER.

1 Timothy 5:8
If anyone does not provide for his relatives,
and especially for his immediate family, he has
denied the faith and is worse than an unbeliever.

LIVE BY A BUDGET AND DON'T FUDGE IT.

Luke 14:28
Suppose one of you wants to build a tower.
Will he not first sit down and estimate the cost
to see if he has enough money to complete it?

LOVEY DOVEY ALLOW; HANKY PANKY ONLY WITH A VOW.

1 Thessalonians 4:7
For God did not call us to be impure,
but to live a holy life.

NEVER MISS A GOOD-BYE KISS.

Song of Songs 4:11
Your lips drop sweetness
as the honeycomb, my bride.

AVOID THE SNARE OF HAVING AN AFFAIR.

Proverbs 5:20
Why be captivated, my son, by an adulteress?
Why embrace the bosom of another man's wife?

BE GENDER TENDER.

Colossians 3:19
Husbands, love your wives
and do not be harsh with them.

TELL YOUR BEAUTY SHE'S A CUTIE.

Song of Songs 4:7
All beautiful you are, my darling;
there is no flaw in you.

SHARE GOD'S TRUTH AND VALUES WITH YOUTH.

Psalm 71:17
Since my youth, O God, you have taught me,
and to this day I declare your marvelous deeds.

LET YOUR HEART SOFTEN MORE OFTEN.

1 Corinthians 13:4
Love is patient, love is kind.
It does not envy, it does not boast,
it is not proud.

LEARN A LOT
BEFORE TYING THE KNOT.

Proverbs 18:22
He who finds a wife finds what is
good and receives favor from the LORD.

CUDDLE ON THE COUCH, AND DON'T BE A GROUCH.

Proverbs 29:22
An angry man stirs up dissension,
and a hot-tempered one commits many sins.

TRY TO MINGLE MORE AS A SINGLE.

Philemon 1:6
I pray that you may be active in sharing your faith,
so that you will have a full understanding
of every good thing we have in Christ.

FORGIVE A FAKE HEADACHE.

1 Corinthians 7:5
Do not deprive each other except by mutual consent
and for a time, so that you may devote yourselves to prayer.

DON'T LET THE SUN GO DOWN IF ANGER IS STILL AROUND.

Ephesians 4:26
In your anger do not sin:
Do not let the sun go down
while you are still angry.

TELL THOSE YOU RARELY TELL YOU LOVE THEM VERY WELL.

Galatians 5:14
The entire law is summed
up in a single command:
"Love your neighbor as yourself."

DON'T DEVOTE YOUR SOUL TO THE REMOTE CONTROL.

Psalm 119:37
Turn my eyes away from worthless things;
preserve my life according to your word.

KNOW VALUES ARE CAUGHT MORE THAN THEY'RE TAUGHT.

Job 29:5
...My children were around me.

NEVER NEGLECT
TO RESPECT AND PROTECT.

1 Peter 3:7
...Be considerate as you live with your wives,
and treat them with respect.

TRAIN CHILDREN AND SHOW THE WAY THEY SHOULD GO.

Proverbs 22:6
Train a child in the way he should go,
and when he is old he will not turn from it.

PUT YOUR SPOUSE FIRST
FOR BETTER OR FOR WORSE.

Ephesians 5:25
Husbands, love your wives,
just as Christ loved the church
and gave himself up for her.

BE TENDER YET BOLD LEADING YOUR HOUSEHOLD.

Joshua 24:15
...As for me and my household,
we will serve the LORD.

NEVER BE LATE ON AN ANNIVERSARY DATE.

Ecclesiastes 9:9
Enjoy life with your wife,
whom you love....

COACH A TEAM FOR YOUR CHILD'S SELF-ESTEEM.

Colossians 3:21
Fathers, do not embitter your children,
or they will become discouraged.

OVERLOOK FLAWS OF MOTHER-IN-LAWS.

1 Peter 4:9
Offer hospitality to one
another without grumbling.

ENHANCE THE CHANCE OF ROMANCE WITH A DANCE.

Song of Songs 2:16
My lover is mine and I am his;
he browses among the lilies.

ONLY SHARE YOUR BED WITH THE WIFE YOU WED.

Hebrews 13:4
Marriage should be honored by all,
and the marriage bed kept pure....

HONOR THE BAND
ON YOUR LEFT HAND.

Song of Songs 8:6
Place me like a seal over your heart,
like a seal on your arm; for love is as strong
as death, its jealousy unyielding as the grave.
It burns like blazing fire, like a mighty flame.

FORGIVE YOUR MATE WITH A CLEAN SLATE.

Colossians 3:13
Bear with each other and forgive
whatever grievances you may have against
one another. Forgive as the Lord forgave you.

INSTEAD OF DIVORCE
TRY TO STAY THE COURSE.

1 Peter 5:10
And the God of all grace . . . after you have
suffered a little while, will himself restore you and
make you strong, firm and steadfast.

DATE
YOUR MATE.

Song of Songs 2:10
My lover spoke and said to me,
"Arise, my darling, my beautiful one,
and come with me."

BE A QUICK WIPER
OF A DIRTY DIAPER.

Romans 12:12
Be joyful in hope,
patient in affliction,
faithful in prayer.

BE A FAITHFUL LOVER NOT LOOKING FOR ANOTHER.

Matthew 19:6
So they are no longer two, but one.
Therefore what God has joined
together, let man not separate.

BEFORE BILLS ARE PAID, TITHE ON EVERY DOLLAR MADE.

Proverbs 3:9
Honor the LORD with your wealth,
with the firstfruits of all your crops.

MAKE YOUR KIDS GLAD YOU'RE THEIR DAD.

Ephesians 6:4
Fathers, do not exasperate your children;
instead, bring them up in the training
and instruction of the LORD.

COMMIT YOUR LOVE LIFE
TO ONLY YOUR WIFE.

Ephesians 5:33
However, each one of you also
must love his wife as he loves himself....

LET THE WORD REVEAL WHAT EVIL TRIES TO STEAL.

Psalm 119:130
The unfolding of your words gives light;
it gives understanding to the simple.

NEVER SKIP PRAISE AND WORSHIP.

1 Chronicles 16:9
Sing to him, sing praise to him;
tell of all his wonderful acts.

STUDY A SERMON THAT HAD YOU SQUIRMIN'.

2 Timothy 4:2
Preach the Word; be prepared in season
and out of season; correct, rebuke and encourage –
with great patience and careful instruction.

PRAY FOR MEN AGAIN AND AGAIN.

Colossians 1:9
For this reason, since the day we heard about you,
we have not stopped praying for you and asking
God to fill you with the knowledge of his will
through all spiritual wisdom and understanding.

HONOR
YOUR PASTOR.

1 Timothy 5:17
The elders who direct the affairs of the church
well are worthy of double honor, especially
those whose work is preaching and teaching.

ONCE A WEEK REST FOR GOD'S BEST.

Deuteronomy 5:12
Observe the Sabbath day by keeping it holy,
as the LORD your God has commanded you.

TAKE TIME TO RELAX AND TUNE OUT WHAT DISTRACTS.

Isaiah 26:3 KJV
Thou wilt keep him in perfect peace,
whose mind is stayed on thee:
because he trusteth in thee.

MINISTER WITH CHARACTER.

2 Timothy 4:5
But you, keep your head in all situations,
endure hardship, do the work of an evangelist,
discharge all the duties of your ministry.

BUILD YOUR LIFE ON LAND FILLED WITH ROCK INSTEAD OF SAND.

Matthew 7:24,25
"Therefore everyone who hears these words of mine
and puts them into practice is like a wise man
who built his house on the rock."

KEEP MEETING TOGETHER, NO MATTER THE WEATHER.

Hebrews 10:25
Let us not give up meeting together,
as some are in the habit of doing,
but let us encourage one another....

RESIST THE ENEMY AND HE WILL FLEE.

James 4:7
Submit yourselves, then, to God.
Resist the devil, and he will flee from you.

BUILD UP ONE ANOTHER, BROTHER TO BROTHER.

Ecclesiastes 4:9,10
Two are better than one, because they have a good return
for their work: If one falls down, his friend can help him up.
But pity the man who falls and has no one to help him up!

AGREE
IN UNITY.

Psalm 133:1
How good and pleasant it is
when brothers live together in unity!

NEVER KILL ANOTHER ENEMY OR BROTHER.

Deuteronomy 5:17 KJV
Thou shall not kill.

AVOID THE POSITION
OF SELFISH AMBITION.

Philippians 2:3
Do nothing out of selfish ambition
or vain conceit, but in humility consider
others better than yourselves.

DON'T BE THE TYPE TO GRUMBLE OR GRIPE.

Philippians 2:14
Do everything without
complaining or arguing.

COMMIT
AND SUBMIT.

Ephesians 5:21
Submit to one another
out of reverence for Christ.

DON'T WAVER DOING A FAVOR.

Romans 15:2
Each of us should please his neighbor
for his good, to build him up.

NEVER JUDGE BY RACE OR BY COLOR OF A FACE.

Romans 14:13
Therefore let us stop passing judgment on one
another. Instead, make up your mind not to put any
stumbling block or obstacle in your brother's way.

AT TIMES BE BLUNT AND CONFRONT.

Proverbs 27:5
Better is open rebuke
than hidden love.

REACH OUT IN GRACE REGARDLESS OF RACE.

1 John 4:21
And he has given us this command:
Whoever loves God must also love his brother.

NEVER CHOOSE TO FALSELY ACCUSE.

Proverbs 3:30
Do not accuse a man for no reason—
when he has done you no harm.

AVOID THE GRIEF
OF BEING A THIEF.

Deuteronomy 5:19 KJV
Neither shalt thou steal.

DON'T OFFEND A FRIEND.

Proverbs 15:1
A gentle answer turns away wrath,
but a harsh word stirs up anger.

BE PURE AND ENDURE.

2 Corinthians 7:1
Since we have these promises, dear
friends, let us purify ourselves from everything
that contaminates body and spirit, perfecting
holiness out of reverence for God.

BE SINCERE WITH A TEAR.

Romans 12:15
Rejoice with those who rejoice;
mourn with those who mourn.

MAKE COMPASSION YOUR FASHION.

Job 29:12,13
...I rescued the poor who cried for help, and the fatherless who had none to assist him. The man who was dying blessed me; I made the widow's heart sing.

DON'T ALWAYS GO WITH THE STATUS QUO.

Colossians 2:8
See to it that no one takes you captive through
hollow and deceptive philosophy, which depends
on human tradition and the basic principles
of this world rather than on Christ.

NEVER FOCUS
ON HOCUS POCUS.

2 Corinthians 11:14
And no wonder, for Satan himself
masquerades as an angel of light.

SEIZE THE DAY
AND DON'T DELAY.

Ephesians 5:16,17
. . . making the most of every opportunity,
because the days are evil. Therefore do not be
foolish, but understand what the LORD'S will is.

SET YOURSELF APART WITH A SERVANT'S HEART.

Matthew 20:26,27
...Whoever wants to become great
among you must be your servant.

WORK WITH GODLY WISDOM IN THE WORLDLY SYSTEM.

Hosea 14:9
Who is wise? He will realize these things.
Who is discerning? He will understand them.
The ways of the LORD are right; the righteous
walk in them, but the rebellious stumble in them.

MAKE DECISIONS BASED ON VISIONS.

Proverbs 29:18 KJV
Where there is no vision,
the people perish....

SET YOUR AMBITION ON THE GREAT COMMISSION.

Matthew 28:19,20
Therefore go and make
disciples of all nations....

HAVE AN ATTITUDE
OF GRATITUDE.

1 Thessalonians 5:18
Give thanks in all circumstances....

WALK
YOUR TALK.

Luke 9:23
If anyone would come after me,
he must deny himself and take up
his cross daily and follow me.

DON'T BE A JERK WHILE AT WORK.

Colossians 3:23
Whatever you do,
work at it with all your heart,
as working for the LORD, not for men.

BE A FRUITFUL HOST
OF THE HOLY GHOST.

Galatians 5:22,23
But the fruit of the Spirit is love, joy,
peace, patience, kindness, goodness,
faithfulness, gentleness and self-control.

SHARE SOME OF YOUR INCOME.

Malachi 3:10
Bring the whole tithe into the storehouse...
and see if I will not throw open
the floodgates of heaven....

WITNESS AND SHARE IN WORD, DEED AND PRAYER.

Mark 16:15
Go into all the world and preach
the good news to all creation.

FOLLOW AND FIGHT WITH SPIRIT INSIGHT.

Zechariah 4:6
"Not by might nor by power,
but by my Spirit," says the LORD Almighty.

TELL THE STORY OF GOSPEL GLORY.

Romans 10:17
Consequently, faith comes from hearing
the message, and the message is heard
through the word of Christ.

BE A SUCCESS
AT DOING YOUR BEST.

2 Timothy 2:15
Do your best to present yourself to God as one
approved, a workman who does not need to be
ashamed and who correctly handles the word of truth.

DON'T CONFORM TO THE WORLDLY NORM.

Romans 12:2
Do not conform any longer to the pattern
of this world, but be transformed
by the renewing of your mind.

GRACE OF HEARTS™
How To Have A Home In Heaven

PLACE
GOD HAS A *PLACE* FOR US IN HEAVEN WHEN WE TRUST.
JOHN 14:2 IN MY FATHER'S HOUSE ARE MANY ROOMS; IF IT WERE NOT SO, I WOULD HAVE TOLD YOU. I AM GOING THERE TO PREPARE A PLACE FOR YOU.

SPACE
SIN HAS PUT A *SPACE* BETWEEN MAN AND GOD'S FACE.
ROMANS 3:23 FOR ALL HAVE SINNED AND HAVE COME SHORT OF THE GLORY OF GOD.

CHASE
MAN *CHASES* AFTER THE WIND WITH A HEART OF SIN.
ECCLESIASTES 1:14 I HAVE SEEN ALL THE THINGS THAT ARE DONE UNDER THE SUN; ALL OF THEM ARE MEANINGLESS, A CHASING AFTER THE WIND.

ERASE
GOD GAVE US HIS ONLY SON TO *ERASE* SIN FOR EVERYONE.

JOHN 3:16 FOR GOD SO LOVED THE WORLD THAT HE GAVE HIS ONE AND ONLY SON, THAT WHOEVER BELIEVES IN HIM SHALL NOT PERISH BUT HAVE ETERNAL LIFE.

GRACE

GOD'S *GRACE* GIVEN TO MAN IS HIS ETERNAL LIFE PLAN.
EPHESIANS 2:8 FOR IT IS BY GRACE YOU HAVE BEEN SAVED THROUGH FAITH - AND THIS NOT FROM YOURSELVES, IT IS THE GIFT OF GOD.

EMBRACE

CONFESS SIN AND BELIEVE; *EMBRACE* JESUS AND RECEIVE.
ROMANS 10:9 IF YOU CONFESS WITH YOUR MOUTH, "JESUS IS LORD," AND BELIEVE IN YOUR HEART THAT GOD RAISED HIM FROM THE DEAD, YOU WILL BE SAVED.

REPLACE

GOD *REPLACES* OUR SIN, THEN NEW LIFE IN CHRIST BEGINS.
2 CORINTHIANS 5:17 THEREFORE, IF ANYONE IS IN CHRIST, HE IS A NEW CREATION; THE OLD HAS GONE, THE NEW HAS COME.

by Cyrano De Words-u-lac
copyright Rhymeo Ink
(540)989-0592

A TALE TO KNOW BY CYRANO
THE INSPIRATION BEHIND A LEGEND
IN HIS OWN RHYME

LET ME SHARE WITH YOU A TALE OF INSPIRATION AND BETRAYAL,
A STORY OF POETIC WORD, OF MY GREAT, GREAT GRANDDAD
CYRANO DE BERGERAC.
FOR HE HAD A TENDER HEART AND HIS NOSE WAS A WORK OF ART,
AS A POET THE PART HE PLAYED WAS THAT OF A ROMANTIC SERENADE.
WHILE ANOTHER MAN SPOKE HIS PROSE, GRANDDAD HID BEHIND HIS NOSE,
AS THE MAIDEN WAS SWAYED BY THE RHYME OF HIS FRIEND'S CHARADE.
GENERATIONS LATER I FOUND OUT ABOUT THIS HOAX BEHIND HIS SNOUT,
AND AS A YOUTH I FELT BETRAYED BY HIS PHONY MASQUERADE.
I BECAME ASHAMED OF THIS MIMICRY AND THE HERITAGE OF MY FAMILY,
BUT THEN ONE DAY I READ BY CHANCE, THE WORDS HE USED FOR ROMANCE.
IT WAS THEN WHEN MY HEART REALIZED THE LEGACY OF MY FAMILY TIES.
I SAW HIM IN A NEW LIGHT. MY HEART WAS TOUCHED, AND NOW I WRITE.
THE PROSE COMPOSED FROM MY PEN, I PROPOSE AS A NEW TREND ...
POETIC PROVERBS KNOWN AS RHYMEOS™, BY THE SHOW-IT POET™ CYRANO,
REARRANGED ALONG THIS PATH OF FAME, WAS MY GRANDDAD'S LAST NAME,
NO LONGER AM I CALLED DE BERGERAC; I AM CYRANO DE WORDS-U-LAC.
IF YOU FIND YOUR LINES ARE FEW, THE WORDS YOU LACK I'LL CHOOSE FOR YOU.
FOR I'VE PLEDGED TO BECOME OVER TIME ... A LEGEND IN MY OWN RHYME.

WHO IS CYRANO?

A LITERARY DIGNITARY	A PROLIFIC WRITER AND POETIC RECITER
A WORD WEAVER RHYMEO™ RETRIEVER	AMONG SUPERMEN OF THE FOUNTAIN PEN

CYRANO DE WORDS-U-LAC

IS THE COMBINED PEN NAME OF BROTHERS
DR. DAN THE MAN & DAVE THE WAVE DAVIDSON

PARTNERS IN RHYME
THE BROTHERS BEHIND CYRANO'S MIND

MORE RHYMEO™ TITLES
by Cyrano De Words-u-lac

It's Time Again To Skip
A Birthday When

A Mother's Love Is Made Up Of

If I Could Live My Life Again

Diamond Dreams

If you have a Rhymeo™ for Cyrano
send what you've penned to the
Quill Guild™